I0606067

ANIMAL
ARCHITECTS

Timothy J. Bradley

Consultants

Timothy Rasinski, Ph.D.
Kent State University

Lori Oczkus
Literacy Consultant

Tejdeep Kochhar
High School Biology Teacher

Based on writing from
TIME For Kids. TIME For Kids and the *TIME
For Kids* logo are registered trademarks of
TIME Inc. Used under license.

Publishing Credits

Dona Herweck Rice, *Editor-in-Chief*
Lee Aucoin, *Creative Director*
Jamey Acosta, *Senior Editor*
Heidi Fiedler, *Editor*
Lexa Hoang, *Designer*
Stephanie Reid, *Photo Editor*
Rane Anderson, *Contributing Author*
Rachelle Cracchiolo, *M.S.Ed., Publisher*

Image Credits: p.23 (bottom) Alamy;
pp.27 (bottom), p.30 Corbis; pp.12–13
(top, middle), p.34 (bottom) Getty Images;
pp.9, 24–25, 48 Timothy J. Bradley; pp.7
(bottom), 11 (middle), 15 (top), 17 (bottom),
39 Photo Researchers, Inc.; p.7 (middle)
REUTERS/Newscom; All other images from
Shutterstock.

Teacher Created Materials

5301 Oceanus Drive
Huntington Beach, CA 92649-1030
http://www.tcmpub.com
ISBN 978-1-4333-4822-8

TABLE OF CONTENTS

NATURE'S BUILDERS

Humans build everything from **spectacular** skyscrapers to tiny tents. Around the world, people build **shelters** to protect them from weather and danger. The best buildings make people feel safe and secure.

Animals are builders, too. Some, such as snails, use their bodies to build a shelter. Others use the scraps they find around them.

For those who know where to look, the homes built in nature are as amazing as human cities. Travel underground to explore an ant city. Step inside to investigate a busy beehive. And discover the secret **dams** beavers build wherever they go. Even in the wild, there's no place like home.

Animal Architects

An **architect** is someone who designs and plans houses, skyscrapers, and other buildings. Animals don't plan their work in the same way humans do, but they still need safe places to live. As they work to stay safe, many animals create stunning structures.

There are over 1,300,000 different types of animals in the world!

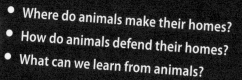

THINK LINK

- Where do animals make their homes?
- How do animals defend their homes?
- What can we learn from animals?

HOMES AT SEA

About 70 percent of Earth is covered in water. Most of that water is in the oceans. Animal life in the ocean is **diverse.** There are more than 200,000 species that live in the ocean. Every species has a unique home.

Just like humans, animals want a home that will keep them safe. The ocean is a big place. And, there is plenty of room for every creature. But it is a dangerous place. Every creature must protect itself from **predators**.

Scientists believe life began in water. Perhaps the first animal homes were built in water.

2010 Marine Census

The Marine **Census** is a collection of information about the ocean. It took 10 years and more than 2,700 scientists to create it. But now we can learn about all the plants and animals that have been discovered in the ocean. The Census tells us where each species lives and how many there are. The ocean is so large that scientists are still finding new species to add to the list.

The yeti crab was discovered in the 2010 Marine Census.

Marine Census scientists named the Dumbo octopus for its fins that look like ears.

CHAMBERED NAUTILUS

The chambered nautilus is related to the octopus and squid. Like its relatives, it has many arms—up to 90! But the nautilus has something the others don't have. It has a beautiful shell that protects it from predators. The shell offers **camouflage**. The top of the shell is dark. It blends in with the dark sea. It is light on the bottom. This blends in with the light coming from above the water. The shell is divided inside. New rooms, or **chambers**, are added to the shell as the animal grows. The nautilus can pull itself inside the shell if it feels threatened.

Protection from Predators

The nautilus's hard shell offers protection from the sharp teeth of predators. Snails and hermit crabs also use shells for protection. In this same way, humans once built walls around castles. These tall rock walls protected the people inside the castle from arrows and cannons.

Clever Colors

From Above

The top of the shell is dark and blends in with the dark sea.

From the Side

The nautilus's blended colors hide it from predators swimming above and below.

From Below

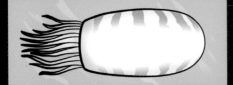

The shell is light on the bottom and blends in with the light coming from above the water.

The nautilus's shell is made up of many chambers.

HERMIT CRABS

Hermit crabs don't have a hard shell like other crabs. Hermit crabs must find an empty shell. They may use a snail's old shell for protection. Their legs grip the shell. When a predator attacks a hermit crab, it pulls its entire body into the shell.

When a human family grows, it moves into a larger house. As the hermit crab grows, its "house" can become too small. The crab must go in search of a new, larger shell. It may even choose a piece of wood or a tin can. If there are not enough empty homes nearby, hermit crabs may fight over a shell.

This hermit crab's shell is covered with anemones.

Finding a New Home

Would you rather live in a house, an apartment, a castle, or a spaceship? Well, hermit crabs have a favorite place to live, too. They prefer snail shells. But if they can't find a snail shell, they will use other types of shells.

snail shell

plastic bottle

conch shell

STICKLEBACKS

Sticklebacks are small fish. They live in oceans and freshwater. The name refers to the sharp spines sticking out from their backs. They don't have scales like other fish.

To attract a female, male sticklebacks build a nest. They make it out of water plants. They use a sticky fluid made in their kidneys to hold it together. The nest attracts females, who lay their eggs there. The nest hides the eggs from predators. Once the eggs hatch, the male keeps looking after the babies. When they are old enough, the babies will swim out on their own.

stickleback nest

Sticklebacks can have anywhere from 2 to 16 spines on their back.

Extended Family

Sticklebacks are cousins to seahorses and pipefish. All three usually have long snouts and small mouths.

HOMES ON LAND

Land offers animals many places to call home. They can build their homes in plants. They may choose trees, bushes, or shrubs. Some animals find shelter in caves. Others live between rocks.

There are nearly as many kinds of animal homes as there are animals. Walking stick bugs live on tree branches and between leaves. Groundhogs dig tunnels. They **burrow** underground in open fields or along roadsides. Sometimes there is not enough space for every animal. Human homes and businesses are taking up more room. They are moving into areas that animals call home.

Mother foxes dig dens in the ground to have their pups.

Walking stick bugs sleep where they are safest—on sticks!

Prairie dogs build underground burrows.

Turtles dig a hole to keep their eggs safe.

SPIDERS

Many types of spiders weave complex webs to catch their **prey**. Spiders make their webs from a special kind of silk. The silk is made in the **spinnerets**. These organs are located on the underside of the abdomen. Spiders can spin different kinds of silk for different uses. Some threads are sticky. Others are not. Some spider silk is used for wrapping prey. Some webs are small. Other webs can be large enough to catch birds. Some spiders even build their webs in an underground tunnel.

Strong as Steel

Imagine holding a thin thread of spider silk. You would have about as much luck pulling that thread apart as you would pulling apart a thread of steel. Although it feels soft to the touch, it is impossible to rip apart.

The spinnerets produce the silk.

Dinnertime

If a spider doesn't catch any prey, it may eat its own web at the end of the day. The silk can be used to build a web another day.

17

Wild Weavers

Spiders have been spinning webs for 140 million years. Different types of spiders spin different kinds of webs. There are orb weavers, funnel weavers, sheet weavers, and more.

Orb Weavers

Orb weavers spin spiral-shaped webs. These types of webs are commonly found in gardens, forests, and fields. When prey is caught in the web, it is quickly bitten and wrapped in silk.

Funnel Weavers

Funnel weavers spin webs in the shape of funnels. The web is spun over animal burrows. When prey is caught in the web, it is pulled into the funnel of the web and eaten.

Sheet Weavers

Spiders hide under a sheet of silk, waiting for prey to fall. When it does, the spider bites the prey through the web and pulls it under. Later, the spider will patch up that part of the web.

GORILLAS

Gorillas are one of the closest living relatives to humans. Each night, we sleep in beds. At that same time, gorillas build a nest for sleeping. The nest is made from the plants and vines the gorillas gather. The nests can be on the ground or up in a tree. The nests give the gorillas a comfortable place to spend the night. Adult gorillas build their own nests. Baby gorillas sleep with their mothers for the first few years. Young gorillas learn how to build nests from their mothers.

a mother and baby gorilla in their nest

Nest Numbers

Scientists count the number of gorilla nests as a way to guess how many gorillas may be in the area. The nests are easier to spot than the gorillas!

Neighborhood Nests

Gorillas aren't the only apes to build nests. Chimpanzees, bonobos, and orangutans also build nests. Sometimes, apes reuse nests built by other apes.

BEAVERS

Beavers live in streams, rivers, and marshes. They build wooden dams. The dams keep predators away from their homes. The beavers pack mud around the outside. In the winter, the mud hardens. The predators cannot get through.

Beavers build their home, or **lodge**, a short distance from the dam. The entrance is hidden underwater. The secret entrance helps beavers avoid predators. A body of water, such as a pond, forms behind the dam. These calmer waters make it easier and safer for the beavers to leave their nest.

Go Long!

The largest beaver dam, located in Alberta, Canada, is 2,790 feet long! That is almost as long as eight football fields!

Tough Teeth

When humans build a house, they use saws to cut through wood. Beavers have a sharp set of front teeth that can easily cut through trees. The front teeth are always growing, so they are always sharp.

Beavers prepare a tree for cutting.

A beaver packs mud and sticks onto the lodge.

DIG DEEPER!

Building the Perfect Lodge

The dam hides the beaver's home. But how do the beavers build a lodge? They work together!

A beaver lodge includes an eating chamber, a sleeping chamber, a place to store food, and canals for moving materials.

1.

The beavers find a large river and use their sharp teeth to cut down trees for logs.

2.

The crew works together to position the cut trees. They create a dam, layering the logs to block the flow of the river.

3.

Nearby, the beavers layer trees to create a frame for the lodge.

4. The family gathers twigs and stones. These are stuck into the holes in between the trees.

5. The beaver uses its broad, flat tail to slap mud down into a thick layer over the twigs and trees.

6. The beaver swims underwater and chews through the branches to make an entrance to the lodge.

TERMITES

Termites are tiny insects that live together in large colonies. Some termites build nests in trees. They dig into the tree to avoid harsh weather and predators. Termites in Africa and Australia build huge, strong mounds. They use soil, **saliva**, and **dung** to make a tall mound. The mounds look solid, but air can easily flow in and out.

Termites store food in the mound. But they don't live in it. Tunnels lead underground into a nest. This is where the termites live. The tunnels keep the inside cool.

Some termites build nests in trees.
Others live underground.

Insect Skyscrapers

The mounds built by termites can be up to 30 feet high! Some areas in Africa have such large mounds that they can be seen by satellite.

A Closer Look

Termite colonies use special chambers for storing eggs, eating, and protecting the queen.

Workers surround this termite queen.

queen

THE BEST OF THE BEST

Animals build homes around the world. Scientists and architects are inspired by the ways animals build their homes. Here are some of our most famous buildings.

Willis Tower

Located in Chicago, Illinois, this skyscraper is 110 stories tall. It has enough offices for about 12,000 workers. The building is covered in aluminum and glass panels.

The Pyramids

The pyramids were built by ancient Egyptians. They were designed to be a special burial place for kings. They were built from big piles of dirt covered with rocks.

The Colosseum

The Colosseum is in Rome, Italy. It is an amphitheater, like a football stadium. It's made of concrete, marble, and limestone.

STOP! THINK...

- Can you see how architects use math to create these buildings?

- Which building do you think is most like an animal building?

- If you were an architect, what kind of building would you design?

Eiffel Tower

The Eiffel Tower is tall enough to be seen from any location in Paris. When the Eiffel Tower was built, nothing like it had ever been created.

The Great Wall of China

The wall was built along China's borders to keep enemies out. The construction took 2,000 years. The wall is so large it can be seen from outer space.

HOMES EVERYWHERE!

People live in all different kinds of places. Some live high in skyscrapers with 100 floors. Others live below ground to avoid the heat. The Inuit people of North America lived in icy **igloos** to survive the cold. Some American Indians built canvas teepees to live in. Today, the Korowai people of Papua build their houses high in the trees. Some of these tree houses are perched 115 feet above the jungle floor!

This tree house in Papua lets people easily watch for danger.

These igloos are made of ice and snow but kept Inuit people in Alaska warm.

Animals make their homes in unexpected places, too. Lions live in the dry Kalahari desert. Polar bears wander through the Arctic **tundra**. Birds and snakes live in jungle trees. Rabbits and foxes live underground. Even though these animals live in places with extreme conditions, they can still build safe homes.

Living underground provides protection for many animals.

BIRDS

Human parents set up a **nursery** for a new baby. They buy a crib and plenty of diapers. Just like humans, each species of bird knows how to build the best kind of nest for its babies. A bird's nest is built to shelter the baby birds from bad weather. The nest should also be difficult for predators to reach. Birds use things like twigs and grass to build a nest for their eggs. They weave a strong nest using just their beaks and their feet. Females are the nest builders in most bird species. But, in some species, males help to build the nest.

The size of a bird's nest can tell you something about the bird's size. Smaller birds make smaller nests and larger birds make larger nests.

Neat Nests

Different kinds of birds build different kinds of nests. Nests can vary from a **shallow** dugout in the sand to mounds of soil and plants. Others build underground burrows or hanging **pendant** nests. Some birds even use mud to build their nests against walls.

Nest Hunters

Some people collect nests. One good way to find a nest is to follow a bird. If you see a bird traveling back and forth, it is probably bringing supplies to its nest. If you find a nest with eggs or birds in it, you should look, but don't touch it!

shallow nest

pendant nest

burrow nest

Seasonal Dwellings

One main reason animals build homes
is to prepare for the changing seasons.
Some need a safe, warm place to spend the winter.
Others want to escape the hot sun in summer.

Fall
Chipmunks dig burrows to keep warm and store food for the winter months.

Winter
Bears can go as long as 100 days without eating or drinking while they hibernate in their den.

Summer
Prairie dogs escape the summer heat in their burrows.

Spring
In the spring, birds often build nests before they lay their eggs.

HONEYBEES

These insects can be found buzzing through gardens around the world. Bees carry **nectar** and **pollen** from the flowers back to their hive. There, it is made into honey. As they fly between the flowers, pollen is carried back and forth. The bees pollinate the flowers. This helps new plants grow.

Bees build elaborate hives. This is where a **colony** can live for years. The hives are filled with six-sided chambers. Honey is made in the upper part of the hive. The center part of it is filled with cells where new bees are born and grow. Queen bees are raised in special chambers called *queen cups*. Bees often use sheltered areas to build their hives. They may build them in holes in trees or even electrical boxes.

Man—made Beehives

Humans have been building beehives for thousands of years. These hives provide easy access to honey. Temples from ancient Egypt show drawings of workers removing honey from hives. Modern hives are built so that the honey can be removed without damaging the hive.

Many people use honey to ease a sore throat when they have a cold.

MOLES

Moles are small mammals that live underground. Moles have developed many **adaptations** for life in the ground. Their big claws are perfect for digging through the soil. Their eyes and ears are tiny. There isn't much to see or hear underground. Moles are able to live with less oxygen. Air is in short supply underground. Living deep in the earth keeps the nearly blind moles safe from predators.

Sound Familiar?

Have you ever heard someone say, "You're making a mountain out of a molehill"? It means you are turning a small problem into a big problem. Most molehills are under two feet tall.

Inside the Molehill

Some tunnels have separate wet and dry areas so that moles can find drinking water during dry times.

There is usually a main tunnel with smaller tunnels branching off.

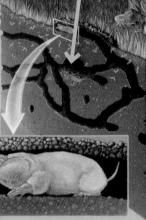

Moles add on to their tunnels year by year to create larger hunting areas.

Slimy Snack

Earthworms are a favorite food of moles. The mole's saliva contains a chemical that **paralyzes** the earthworms but doesn't kill them. Moles carve out underground **larders**. They store the paralyzed earthworms inside until they are ready to eat them.

IMPORTANT INSTINCTS

Some animals use their bodies as houses. Other animals work together to build a safe place to live. It takes years for humans to learn how to build houses. But animals are born knowing how. They build their homes by **instinct**. They know how to find the right materials and put them together. Around the world, scientists are studying these amazing animals to see what they can teach human architects.

beaver lodge

termite mound

beehive

GLOSSARY

adaptations—traits that have developed in animals and plants to help them survive in their habitat

architect—a person who designs buildings

burrow—to tunnel or dig

camouflage—color or texture that helps a plant or animal blend into its environment

census—an official counting of the population

chambers—enclosed spaces

colony—a group of organisms of the same type living together

dams—barriers preventing the flow of water

diverse—a number of things or creatures differing from one another

dung—solid animal waste

igloos—dome-shaped houses made of blocks of snow and ice

instinct—natural abilities and responses

larders—places to store food

lodge—a beaver's home

nectar—a sweet liquid found in flowers

nursery—a baby's bedroom

paralyzes—makes something unable to move

pendant—something that hangs down

pollen—a yellow, powdery substance produced by plants in order to reproduce

predators—animals that kill and eat other animals

prey—organisms that are consumed by others for energy

saliva—a fluid made by the mouth

shallow—not deep

shelters—places that house and protect animals

spectacular—exciting to see

spinnerets—specialized organs a spider uses to produce silk for webs

tundra—a treeless arctic area

INDEX

BIBLIOGRAPHY

Caney, Steven. *Steve Caney's Ultimate Building Book.* Running Press Kids, 2006.

This book is filled with easy-to-make projects that help kids understand architecture and construction.

Robinson, W. Wright. *Animal Architects How Insects Build Their Amazing Homes.* Blackbirch Press, 1999.

Learn all about how insects such as bees, termites, and ants construct their homes. Some homes are simple, and others are very complex.

Salvadori, Mario, Saralinda Hooker, and Christopher Ragus. The Art of Construction: Projects and Principles for Beginning Engineers and Architects. Chicago Review Press, 2000.

Learn about the basic principles of building and architecture in this book written for kids ages 10 and up. Instructions for using everyday materials to build basic structures are also included.

Stonehouse, Bernard, and Esther Bertram. *The Truth About Animal Builders.* Tangerine Press, 2003.

Discover the secrets and myths about animal builders. Learn how and why animals fit into categories based on how they build places to live.

MORE TO EXPLORE

National Geographic Really Wild Animals Awesome Animal Builders DVD

This video follows many different animal builders and investigates the special tools they use to build their homes.

ArchKIDecture

http://www.archkidecture.org/

ArchKIDecture is a website that was created to explain architecture, as well as math, science, and visual arts.

Encyclopedia Britannica for Kids

http://kids.britannica.com/

Encyclopedia Britannica Online provides a searchable database of information on any content you are studying in class or that you would like to know more about, including bugs. Encyclopedia entries are written for kids ages 8–11 or 11 and up.

BioKids

http://biokids.umich.edu/guides/tracks_and_sign

Many animals build homes for themselves or their offspring. You might encounter some of these homes in real life. Read about them on this website so you will know what to watch out for.

ABOUT THE AUTHOR

Timothy J. Bradley grew up near Boston, Massachusetts, and spent every spare minute drawing spaceships, robots, and dinosaurs. He enjoyed it so much that he started writing and illustrating books about natural history and science fiction. Timothy also worked as a toy designer for Hasbro, Inc., and designed life-size dinosaurs for museum exhibits. Timothy loves looking at bugs and the amazing things they can build.

Timothy lives in sunny Southern California with his wife and son.